CHANGING LITERACIES: MEDIA EDUCATION AND MODERN CULTURE

THE LONDON FILE - PAPERS FROM THE
INSTITUTE OF EDUCATION
Titles in the series include:

MUSIC EDUCATION AND THE NATIONAL CURRICULUM	Keith Swanwick
WHAT WE KNOW ABOUT EFFECTIVE PRIMARY TEACHING	Caroline Gipps
THE ARTS 5-16: Changing the agenda	John White
MORE HAS MEANT WOMEN: The feminisation of schooling	Jane Miller
NATIONAL CURRICULUM SCIENCE: So near and yet so far	Arthur Jennings
THE PROMISE AND PERILS OF EDUCATIONAL COMPARISON	Martin McLean
THE AIMS OF SCHOOL HISTORY: Has the National Curriculum got it right?	Peter Lee, John Slater, Paddy Walsh and John White
TIME TO CHANGE THE 1981 EDUCATION ACT	Brahm Norwich
A MARKET-LED ALTERNATIVE FOR THE CURRICULUM: Breaking the code	James Tooley
PARTNERSHIP IN INITIAL TEACHER TRAINING: Talk and chalk	Clare Hake
EDUCATION AND THE CRISIS IN VALUES: Should we be philosophical about it?	Graham Haydon

THE LONDON FILE
PAPERS FROM THE INSTITUTE OF EDUCATION

CHANGING LITERACIES: MEDIA EDUCATION AND MODERN CULTURE

DAVID BUCKINGHAM

INSTITUTE OF EDUCATION
UNIVERSITY OF LONDON

Published by

the Tufnell Press

THE LONDON FILE - PAPERS FROM THE INSTITUTE OF EDUCATION

PUBLISHED
by
the Tufnell Press
47, Dalmeny Road, London, N7 0DY

All Rights reserved. No part of this publication may be reproduced, stored in a retrieval system, or transmitted in any form or by any means, electronic, mechanical, photocopying, recording or otherwise, without the prior permission of the publisher.

© 1993, David Buckingham

First published 1993

BRITISH LIBRARY CATALOGUING-IN-PUBLICATION DATA
A catalogue record for this book is available from the British Library

ISBN 1 872767 61 3

Book design by Fiona Barlow, Carter Wong, London
Printed in Great Britain by Da Costa Print, London

CONTENTS

CHANGING LITERACIES: MEDIA EDUCATION AND MODERN CULTURE	1
THE CASE FOR MEDIA EDUCATION	3
LITERACY NOW AND IN THE FUTURE	5
TECHNOLOGIES	7
INSTITUTIONS	11
TEXTS	15
AUDIENCES	19
IMPLICATIONS FOR EDUCATION	22
CONCLUSION	26
NOTES AND REFERENCES	28

CHANGING LITERACIES:
MEDIA EDUCATION AND MODERN CULTURE

BAN TRASHY NEIGHBOURS
It makes our kids dunces, says Minister

Top TV soap *Neighbours* should be BANNED because it is 'junk', a Government minister said last night.

Michael Fallon, 39, who is Minister for Schools, claimed the hit Aussie series is turning millions of children into dunces.

He said: 'I would like to see *Neighbours* banned. Children learn nothing from these junk programmes which dull their senses, making teachers' jobs even harder.'

Mr. Fallon, who has two sons aged two-and-a-half and ten months, spoke after a survey revealed that six out of ten youngsters spend more time in front of the telly than in the CLASSROOM.

He added: 'Watching this amount of TV is turning children into passive, unimaginative voyeurs.'[1]

At first sight, it might appear bizarre for a Government Minister, charged with responsibility for the education of millions of children, to spend his time denouncing an Australian soap opera. Yet Michael Fallon's attack on *Neighbours* was merely one instance of what has become a recurrent preoccupation for Tory politicians and educational policy makers in recent years.

What seems to have caused the most outrage, however, is not simply that most children choose to watch this 'junk': it is also that many teachers choose to teach about it. At the Conservative party conference in 1992, for example, Education Minister John Patten ridiculed one examination board for setting a question that involved analysing a hamburger advertisement; while the Prime Minister himself condemned the notion of studying soap opera, promising 'there'll be no GCSE in *Eldorado*'. Meanwhile, NCC Chairman David Pascall has expressed concern about the 'pervasive diet of cartoons, sloppy speech and soap operas' that he sees as undermining the 'cultural development' of young people.[2] And television has also been routinely cited as a major cause of the alleged decline in standards of literacy.

These arguments are of course part of a much more fundamental debate about education and culture which is currently being waged over the English curriculum. The most obvious manifestation of this debate comes in the form of a perennial concern about *cultural value*. Education is seen to play a central role here, in maintaining and policing necessary distinctions between the timeless values of 'art' and 'literature' on the one hand, and the disposable trivia of 'popular culture' on the other. Indeed, if Shakespeare has become the symbolic talisman of cultural value, *Neighbours* has increasingly become the Bad Object in such debates—a phenomenon which is quite implausible, given its sheer inoffensiveness. To be able to claim that one 'has read Shakespeare' seems to serve as an indispensable guarantee of what it means to be a civilised British citizen. By contrast, watching *Neighbours* is condemned as a passive, mindless pursuit, which is at best a waste of time, and at worst a dangerous form of voyeurism. Consuming popular media is seen to require no intellectual or cultural competencies, and thus to develop none.

Yet the threat which seems to be posed by studying popular media in schools derives, not simply from the need to preserve particular 'standards' of cultural value, but from much deeper anxieties about changes in the social order and in the national culture. As in many other areas, the media serve as a convenient scapegoat, an easy explanation for much more complex processes; and the solution is seen to lie in a return to 'traditional values', to a mythical era of social stability and national unity, embodied in the English literary canon. The role of the media in these debates is thus almost wholly negative: they are seen unequivocally as the sworn enemies of literacy, of true culture, and of civilization itself.

In educational terms, this debate sets an extraordinarily narrow agenda, both in terms of *what* young people should read, and in terms of *how* they should read it. Implicitly, we are asked to choose between Shakespeare and *Neighbours*, as if the two were mutually exclusive. And if teaching Shakespeare is about developing students' ability to 'appreciate' what is self-evidently Good, the only possible reason for teaching about *Neighbours* is to develop their ability to 'see through' what is self-evidently Bad, and hence to wean them on to Better Things. In this process, fundamental questions about the *purpose* of teaching about culture come to be defined in increasingly simplistic terms.

The culmination of these debates, and the immediate context for this paper, has been the proposal to remove the statutory elements of media education from the National Curriculum for English—elements which, it should be emphasised, are a comparatively minor aspect of the subject as a whole. In their place is a significantly extended list of literary texts, very few of which could be described as in any way contemporary. In my view, and in the view of most English teachers, this is a recipe for a form of education that will prove increasingly irrelevant to the social worlds in which the vast majority of young people live.

The case for media education

My aim in this paper, then, is partly to make the case for media education as a fundamental educational entitlement for all. The case is, on one level, quite straightforward. If the curriculum is to equip young people to understand and to participate in their society, it must inevitably begin by acknowledging the cultural experiences of the majority. As Paul Willis's book *Common Culture*[3] has recently reminded us, those experiences are decisively not about the traditional arts, or about traditional forms of literacy. This can easily be demonstrated in terms of statistics:

* Only 5 per cent of the UK population, and only 2 per cent of the British working class, attend the theatre, opera or ballet, or visit museums or art galleries.

* Two per cent of all young people, excluding students, attend the theatre, the most popular traditional arts venue.

* Ninety-eight per cent of the population watch television on average for around 23 hours a week.

* Around 90 per cent of young people listen to the radio, primarily for music, or to records or tapes.

* Forty-one per cent of the population, and 60 per cent of working class people, did not read a book of any kind during the last month—and of those who did, it would be interesting to speculate how many of those books would come into the socially-sanctioned category of 'literature' (the best-seller lists would suggest surprisingly few).

To some extent, these statistics could well be seen to fuel the arguments of the political Right—although they might also serve to remind them of the enormity of the task they appear to have set themselves. In this situation, attempting to displace *Neighbours*—regularly watched by the large majority of young people—with the spontaneous appreciation of the works of Shakespeare would seem to be, at the very least, an uphill struggle.

My response to these figures is not to suggest that the situation they reveal is something we should celebrate—any more than it is something we should bemoan and take as evidence of the terminal ignorance and pathological voyeurism of the young. I simply want to argue, at this stage, that we need to recognise the central importance of the media in young people's lives. More broadly, we need to acknowledge that contemporary culture is, by and large, electronically mediated culture; and that many traditional oral or written forms of communication have at least been supplemented, to a large extent changed, and even in some respects displaced, by communication which uses electronic media. It is from the media that we derive the majority of our information about the world, and of our experience of fictional texts; as such, they play a central role in our relationships with our families and friends, and in the processes whereby our identities come to be formed. Yet these are phenomena which the revised English curriculum seems deliberately to ignore.

However, the case for media education is not simply based on notions of 'relevance'. Media education is not a lazy response to the popularity of the media, nor merely an attempt to validate what children already know. On the contrary, it provides a very clear definition of the conceptual understandings that are involved, both in 'reading' and in 'writing' media texts.[4] It is far from being an easy option, either for students or for teachers themselves. As many teachers have begun to acknowledge, media education offers a rigorous theoretical basis for learning about contemporary culture which has a good deal to offer to English, not least to the study of literature.

It is for these reasons that the place of media education within the core subject of English is so important. There is every sign that Media Studies, as a specialist subject, will continue to expand in the upper years of secondary schooling and in further and higher education: the interest and enthusiasm of students and teachers (and indeed of many parents) will ensure it. Yet, for the reasons I have outlined, understanding the media needs to be seen as a central aspect of what it means to be literate in contemporary societies. A substantial and coherent form of media education should be an essential element of schooling for all young people, rather than something that is confined to a minority of specialists.

Literacy now and in the future

In using the term 'literacy' in this context, therefore, I am implicitly making a polemical claim. For many people, the notion of 'media literacy' must represent a contradiction in terms, if not an unholy alliance. Of course, on a theoretical level, the metaphor of media literacy is highly problematic: its value and its usefulness depend to a large extent on how one chooses to define literacy itself. Recent research on literacy has pointed to the need for a broader definition of the term, which acknowledges that it is inevitably embedded within particular social relationships and practices.[5] The nature of literacy—or, more accurately, of literacies—is culturally and historically diverse and changeable: and, as I shall argue, we are currently living in a period, like earlier periods such as the Renaissance, where the pace of change appears to be accelerating. Any contemporary definition of literacy must therefore inevitably include the understandings and competencies that are developed in relation to 'new' media technologies as well as 'older' technologies such as writing and print.

It is for these reasons that I want to move beyond the limitations of the debates I have outlined, and to look to the future. I want to project into the twenty-first century, now less than seven years away, and to ask: what does literacy mean, and what will it mean, for children in schools now, the children who will be coming of age in the next century? And in particular, what forms of literacy will be relevant to the modern popular media which are so central to their experience?

In attempting to answer these questions, I want to suggest that literacy is formed and practised in the interaction between *technologies, institutions, texts* and *audiences*. Historically, different academic paradigms within Media Studies have tended to emphasise certain of these dimensions at the expense of others, and hence to arrive at very different estimations of the 'power' of the media. In the past, much of the power has been seen to lie with media institutions (for example, with broadcasters or publishers) and with the texts they produce: audiences have been assumed simply to absorb the meanings that are imposed upon them. Thus, for example, the media have often been regarded as the major cause of violence, of immorality, of 'consumerism' or of undesirable social attitudes among audiences. More recently, however, there has been a move to an opposite position, in which audiences are seen to possess a considerable degree of autonomy, and the power to create meanings of their own free will. Research has emphasised the very diverse ways in which readers use and make sense of the media: texts which may appear to embody 'conservative' attitudes, for example about male and female roles, may in fact be interpreted in much more 'progressive' or indeed subversive ways by audiences.

My aim here, however, is to stress the *interaction* between these different elements of the process, without conceding a necessary priority to any one of them. The 'power' of the media is not merely a *possession*, whether of institutions, texts or audiences: on the contrary, it is inherent in the *relationships* between them. The question of 'where the power lies' is one that requires empirical answers as much as theoretical ones: and, to this extent, my specific examples are intended to be illustrative rather than definitive. Finally, by employing this conceptual framework, I also hope to indicate some of the kinds of questions that teachers might be asking about contemporary culture, and that students might be encouraged to explore: and it is these *educational* implications to which I shall return in my conclusion.

David Buckingham

Technologies

One familiar way of predicting the future is to look at technology—that is, at the physical resources with which literacy is practised, and the social relations that surround them. This is undoubtedly problematic: technologies do not produce social change, nor are they simply produced by it, as Raymond Williams pointed out many years ago.[6] Nevertheless, they are at least an index of what might be happening.

In defining technology in this way, I am implicitly including the book and the pen (and indeed writing itself) as technologies, as well as the media and computer technologies I shall go on to discuss. If writing or print are technologies, which partly replaced but also blended with those of a previous era, so at this point we are living through a process of massive technological change, in which a similar interaction between technologies is taking place. In this context, attempting to separate 'traditional' and 'modern' technologies, and seeking to identify the 'effects' of each upon the other, may prove increasingly difficult.

These changes are obviously largely a result of developments in micro-computing, or in ways of generating and handling digital information. In particular, I want to discuss the development of *multi-media*—whose growth over the past few years has been extraordinary, and in the next five years is likely to transform cultural production and reception. Multi-media is part of an even broader integration of communication and information media which has been made possible by digital technology. Basically, what multi-media offers is the possibility of transforming different kinds of data (images, sound, text, and so on) into digital information that can be stored and manipulated by the computer. What is significant here is that specialist technologies that were previously extremely expensive are now becoming very much cheaper, and are going to be targeted increasingly at the home consumer.

One example of this is the 'interactive' compact disc, which seems poised to begin a significant move into the domestic market. What this technology enables you to do is to connect up a CD player with a domestic computer. This is important because the CD allows you to store enormous amounts of information of various kinds, and to gain random access to it:

it is possible to store thousands of pages of information, text and colour images, including moving images, as well of course as sound, on a single CD and then gain access in any order or sequence you like.

Despite the arguments of some enthusiasts, this is not immediately going to replace the book. Nevertheless, it is clear that it can do many of the things that you can do with books much more efficiently and easily—such as cross-referencing, reading at your own pace, and choosing your own way through—as well as offering the added benefits of sound and moving images. To date, interactive CDs have been used mainly for encyclopedias and dictionaries, which are primarily about information retrieval, and where their benefits are much more obvious. However, recent work in this field suggests that the technology also possesses considerable potential for generating new artistic and fictional forms. The interactive CD offers very different possibilities in terms of narrative, for example, that move beyond a traditional linear structure—and there are signs that this is beginning to influence the approach of 'older' media, for example in some children's television.

The interactive CD is primarily a 'consumer' technology, in that it offers a way of storing and retrieving existing information. It is 'interactive' only in the sense that it allows the reader to choose different paths through that information—although this in itself significantly changes what is normally meant by consumption, or by reading, at least in relation to moving images. But in many other areas of multi-media, we are seeing a revolution in technology which affected cultural production first, and is now becoming affordable at the level of the domestic consumer.

So, to choose another example, the development of digital sound-recording technology has already revolutionised the music industry, but is now becoming an affordable option for home use. You can now buy for a few hundred pounds a software package which will allow you to connect up an electronic keyboard with a simple computer and then manipulate the sounds at your leisure, using very sophisticated editing techniques. You can sample existing sounds and alter them in terms of pitch and rhythm; you can edit much more precisely than used to be possible using tape and a razor blade; you can lay tracks on top of each other in a way that was previously only possible using very complex and expensive multi-channel mixers; and so on. Over five years, we have moved a very long way from home taping, or from the first electronic keyboards, with their pre-programmed sounds and rhythm tracks.

Another example of multi-media is image manipulation. It is now possible to buy, again for a couple of hundred pounds, a scanner which will enable you to read images and convert them into digital information which can be stored and then manipulated in the computer. This offers endless possibilities for editing, combining, and adapting images for your own purposes. And now, in the last few months, the same has become possible with video images: again, using a comparatively cheap device, you can now achieve many effects that were previously only possible with extremely complex and expensive video editing equipment, such as quantel and paintboxes. There are still problems here with the size of the image, and the amount of computer space that is needed to store the information, but there is no reason to think these will not be overcome. Significantly, these developments build upon technologies that have already become much more accessible for the domestic user: video recorders are now available in something like 75 per cent of homes with children, and despite the recession, around two million portable video camcorders are currently being bought every year, predominantly by families with children, and by no means only by middle class ones.

On one level, then, these technologies could be seen simply as an extension of those which are already widely available. The marketing of 'home video', for example, employs many of the ideological themes which have been developed in marketing still cameras and 'home movies', most notably the emphasis on family harmony. Yet while there is as yet little research, it is clear that the uses of video technology are much more diverse and idiosyncratic than this would suggest. Video permits a much more conscious, and potentially subversive, manipulation of commercially-produced media texts, for example through 'sampling' and re-editing material recorded off-air—and digital multi-media radically extends these possibilities. The large numbers of children now growing up with video will clearly have a very different relationship with broadcast television than the generations that preceded them.

Nevertheless, it is important to retain a degree of scepticism here. There are obvious dangers in talking about technology in isolation. On the one hand, there is the temptation of what we might call the techno-fix—the assumption that technology will solve all social ills, or at least that it makes the difference in itself—which is in effect a form of technological determinism. But on the other hand, there is the danger of techno-phobia—the fear that new technologies will wholly displace traditional technologies, that they will irreparably damage social relationships, and lead to artificial, unnatural behaviour and ways of thinking. Such arguments almost inevitably end up over-estimating the autonomy and power of technology.

For others, there is a slightly different kind of determinism—a fear that technologies are inherently gendered and (perhaps to a lesser extent) determined by social class. For example, there is a common view that computers or videos are 'boys' toys', and that the best response is either outright refusal or a kind of cultural Luddism. These issues are certainly in need of further research. Nevertheless, there are signs that the 'gendering' of these electronic technologies may become much less polarised as they are more widely used; and that the distribution of the technologies, and of the skills and competencies they require, is far from being straightforwardly predictable in terms of social class.

Ultimately, the danger in all these arguments is one of essentialism—of assuming that technologies inherently and inevitably produce certain social relationships, or are produced by them. Again, as Raymond Williams argued,[7] we need a broader sense of the interaction between technology and the socio-cultural context if we are to make sense of where technology might fit and where it might lead.

In moving on, therefore, I want to argue that there are two sets of forces which seem to be pulling in different directions. We might term these centrifugal and centripetal. On the one hand, there are forces pulling away from the centre, towards fragmentation, differentiation, and individualisation. On the other, there are forces reasserting central control, the power of the state or of capital, forces of homogeneity and uniformity. These forces characterise both the macro-level of cultural policy and the micro-level of everyday uses of culture: they function at the level of the global or national and the local or domestic. Many of the developments we are witnessing show a complex combination of these tendencies, and it is for this reason that their political consequences are likely to prove quite contradictory.

This opposition takes us back to debates in the early days of the new media technologies, for example in the work of the Frankfurt School. To put it fairly crudely, what can be found there is a debate between, on the one hand, a pessimistic analysis of popular culture, which sees it as being about homogenisation, massification, and increasing control by centralised elites and by capital; and on the other hand, a more optimistic argument, which sees democratic possibilities in popular culture and in new technologies, possibilities for lateral communication, as opposed to vertical, top-down communication.[8]

For example, these different forces are implicit in the technological developments I have discussed. On the one hand, they seem to emphasise privatised, domestic, individualised practices. Media production and consumption may come to be seen, not as group activities, but rather as something that happens in the isolated interaction between the individual and the screen. In addition, perhaps, they seem to imply a reduction of the public sphere, in favour of a notion of the individual not as a citizen but merely as a consumer of technologies and of information. Equally, on the other hand, they seem to make possible forms of production and consumption which could be described as dialogic, involving the critical and autonomous use of available resources, for example in the form of 'sampling'. In the process, they make a mockery of copyright, of notions of intellectual property and of the power of media institutions. At least potentially, they may enable a democratisation of production that has previously been confined to elites, and a form of control over consumption that is worrying and threatening to those elites—and ultimately perhaps, a blurring of the distinction between production and consumption itself.

Institutions

These contradictions are particularly apparent when one considers the institutional contexts in which communication technologies are produced and used, and the changing patterns of control and regulation, for example of broadcasting or the press. Again, it is important to avoid a kind of determinism here—a tendency which has certainly been characteristic of a good deal of media sociology. Control of the means of production does not necessarily result in control over the production of meaning. The meanings and pleasures readers derive from the media—and indeed the forms of literacy they develop—are not wholly determined by these institutions, although they clearly do exert constraints and create possibilities.

Let us take broadcasting as an example. The past ten years has seen a gradual dismantling of the existing broadcasting system in this country. This has happened as a result of a complex combination of technological, political and economic factors. New (or new-ish) technologies such as cable and satellite have led to a massive proliferation of broadcast channels, with a resulting growth in competition. The existing institutions (both the BBC and the commercial companies) have decreased in size, as production has increasingly shifted to smaller, so-called 'independent' companies—although this has happened primarily as a result of central government directives, which have sought to reduce labour costs and trades union power. The whole pattern of employment in broadcasting has become much more casualised, with far greater reliance on freelance labour. And we have seen the allocation of broadcasting franchises reduced to an essentially commercial affair, in which traditional notions of public service have been very much pushed to the margins.

This is a process which is going to continue for years to come; but it does not take a prophet to predict that the whole shape of broadcasting, and in particular of the BBC, is going to be radically changed within the next three or four years, in the long run-up to the renegotiation of the BBC Charter. What we are seeing here is essentially a move towards a deregulated, much more commercial system, determined by what the Tories are wont to call 'market forces'. In the process, the traditional paternalistic notion of broadcasting as a public service—a notion which was always problematic—has become much harder to sustain.

Nevertheless, it is possible to detect in government policy, and in the debates that surround (for example) the screening of major sporting events or the ITV franchise auction or even in the BBC's rather desperate approach to its doomed soap opera *Eldorado*, a familiar contradiction which has characterised many areas of social policy in the last decade, not least education. On the one hand, we have the move towards the so-called 'free market', towards deregulation, and the predominance of commercial imperatives; while on the other, we have a growing anxiety about the need for state regulation, for sustaining moral standards and centralised control over what people are allowed to see and to know—so we have the Video Recordings Act, and various new regulatory bodies such as the Broadcasting Standards Council, the Broadcasting Complaints Commission, and so on.

At the same time, for all the talk of consumer sovereignty, deregulation cannot automatically be equated with greater choice and diversity. On the contrary, the whole strategy of deregulation, while it appears to undermine the power of existing national institutions, also increases the power of the multinationals—of Murdoch, Berlusconi, Bertelsmann and others. And if the notion of public service, of a single broadcasting system speaking to and for the nation, and with it the notion of a single national culture, is becoming redundant—some would say it always was—it is giving way not merely to internal fragmentation and diversity, but also to internationalisation.

I have used broadcasting as an example here, but one could make similar arguments about the press. The recent debate about privacy and press freedom, which has intensified in the wake of 'Squidgy' and the 'Camillagate' affair, has been characterised by this same contradiction between the demands of the market—or in this case, the tabloids struggling to reverse their decline in circulation—and on the other hand the maintaining of moral standards and public decency. This contradiction between the right to privacy and the right to know is obviously a highly political issue: it is ultimately about the relationship between the rulers and the ruled, about a small group of people whose continuing power and privilege is only possible through our financial support. It is one of the great ironies of the contradictory role of the media that the apparently conservative tabloids have played such a major role in undermining the monarchy, and may well have been instrumental in ensuring its demise.

Nevertheless, as this example suggests, the political consequences of these developments are not easy to identify. On the Left, for example, some of the staunchest critics of public service have rapidly turned round to become its most enthusiastic defenders. Many have argued that the so-called public sphere has been invaded by commerce, and that the role of

...edia as a potential means of ensuring political debate, and even political participation, has been effectively destroyed.[9] Of course, it is debatable whether this notion of the public sphere—this almost utopian idea of free public communication—ever really existed, or whether it can be seen as relevant to complex, contemporary societies; and it is certainly questionable whether public service and the broadcasting duopoly as they have evolved in this country, as an uneasy balance of forces between the market and the state, could ever have really fulfilled this role.

On the other hand, however, there are others—both on the Right and on the Left—who would argue that this abandonment to market forces and this loosening of centralised control has actually resulted in greater democratic possibilities. So, for example, they would point to the way in which cable TV and commercial radio have encouraged the provision of specialist stations for ethnic minority groups, and other social groups who were previously ignored or at least patronised by mainstream media. In addition, one could argue that changing patterns of employment and training within the industries, as well as the increasing availability of cheap production technology, have led to a blurring of the distinctions between amateur and professional production. Perhaps particularly for young people, camcorders, simple audio mixing equipment, and home computers have become easily available means of expression—and this is definitely not just a luxury for the middle classes.[10]

This tendency is certainly apparent in the specialist 'fan cultures' that surround comics, computer games, and obviously popular music, where the distance between 'consumers' and 'producers' is comparatively small.[11] But even in the previously less democratic medium of video and TV, the institutions are having to recognise the democratic potential of the new technology—and this is something that is not merely confined to the likes of Jeremy Beadle. For example, the *Video Diaries* recently shown on BBC2 have included some of the most innovative and thought-provoking television we have seen since the early days of Channel 4.

Nevertheless, the key question here is to what extent any of these things really amounts to a form of democratisation. To what extent are these developments merely a form of tokenism, and how far have the institutions continued to retain control? The experience, for example, of specialist radio stations or of access TV has actually been rather more problematic—and one could make a parallel here with the radio phone-in, which has turned out to be rather less than a democratic force for change.

Texts

The provision of media specifically for children has been one of the key issues in the debates about changes in broadcasting, notably around the renewal of the ITV franchises. Broadcasting for children is traditionally part of the public service remit; and the argument has been that abandoning broadcasting to market forces would result in a reduction of the quality and the amount of children's programming. Broadcasters themselves have argued that children are not a significant enough market for advertisers, so that it will become increasingly impossible to produce, for example, home-grown drama or broadly educative programmes. Instead, what has been threatened is an increased reliance on cheap, bought-in programming, largely from the United States. The example of US children's television—the so-called Kid Vid ghetto—has been held up as indication of the appalling fate that would await us: it is described as a kind of commercial wasteland, in which children are left helpless and unprotected in the face of a barrage of violence, sexism, consumerism and merchandising. A public lobby group—British Action for Children's TV—has been formed to defend the public service tradition, based on an American model: and both groups, perhaps surprisingly, have been relatively successful in ensuring some kind of commitment to children's TV on both sides of the Atlantic.

While these attempts to defend children's programming seem to me to be extremely important, they obviously raise some rather more problematic issues. For example, much of the anxiety is based on a rather partial notion of national identity, and a fear of Americanisation—a fear that has characterised debates about the media and popular culture for much of this century[12] (although, as the debate about *Neighbours* suggests, this may have begun to change more recently into a fear of Australianisation!). These debates also invoke questionable assumptions about the 'effects' of the media on young minds, which are assumed to be vulnerable and impressionable and thus in need of adult protection; and this in turn relates to broader questions about adults' constructions of children and of childhood itself. Cultural value is again another central issue; and there is certainly a sense in which the argument for 'quality' has often been seen as an argument for a very middle class, paternalistic notion of children's TV, in the mould of *Blue Peter* or *The Chronicles of Narnia*. Yet there has been hardly any investigation into what children themselves might define as 'quality', and very little sense in which they have been able to participate in the debate.[13]

These kinds of tensions and anxieties can also be traced in programmes themselves. What is very striking about a lot of British children's television, and particularly magazine format programmes, is how the imperative to 'entertain' and to sustain audiences has increasingly been in tension with the imperative to educate and to inform—a tension which seems to me to result in a good deal of incoherence and superficiality.

At the same time, if you seek out the material which is most popular with younger children—Saturday morning TV, the advertisements, and particularly the cartoons like *Teenage Mutant Ninja Turtles* or *Toxic Crusaders*—what you find is something which to most adults looks extremely bizarre, and probably quite incomprehensible. There are certainly continuities with the kind of material I used to enjoy as a child—with the *Flintstones* or *Thunderbirds* (and, indeed, it is significant that these series are currently being re-run). But what you also find here is a blurring of boundaries, both between texts and between media. The cartoons refer to and draw on other texts, other genres, sometimes in the form of direct quotation or 'sampling'. They raid existing cultural resources—both from high culture and from the popular culture of the past and present—in a fragmentary and often apparently ironic manner.

Yet TV programmes are not just TV programmes: they are also films, comics, computer games and toys—not to mention T-shirts, lunchboxes, drinks, sticker albums, food, and a myriad of other products. What children are exposed to—what they are increasingly participating in—is an elaborate system of intertextuality, a system which crosses the boundaries between traditional media forms. And what they are developing—what they are assumed to possess—is a very particular kind of sophistication, a highly developed form of literacy, which is probably unrecognisable (and unrecognised) by most of us—albeit one which is perhaps inextricably tied to the operations of the market.[14]

Again, I have concentrated on television, but similar arguments might be made about other popular media. For example, one could point to the complex, self-conscious intertextuality of contemporary comics such as *2000 AD* or *Death's Head*[15]; and of some rap music, for example of bands like De La Soul and A Tribe Called Quest. What you find here is an ironic raiding of popular and high culture (in the case of rap music literally through quotation or sampling), the juxtaposition of incongruous elements from different historical periods, different cultural and artistic contexts—in effect, a blurring of the boundaries of time and place. At least in the case of the examples I have mentioned, this is allied to what I would argue is some very sophisticated and witty political commentary.

Indeed, within popular music more broadly, the map has changed in some very interesting ways in the last five years. We have seen a proliferation or an increasing fragmentation of genres and sub-genres, particularly of forms of what might broadly be called dance music. The distinctions between genres like hip-hop, rap, house, techno, acid, ragga, and hardcore (to name but a few) are certainly hard to define for outsiders—although obviously that is partly the point. Indeed, there is now a sense in which genre itself has become much more significant as an organising category, as opposed for example to authors or artists. What is important also is that the definition of genres, the policing of the boundaries, is as much in the hands of audiences as it is of producers: what counts as 'hardcore' rap or 'deep' house is not just what the record company or even the radio station says it is.

Despite the self-conscious and partly ironic resurgence of 'pop' as a genre in the early Eighties, the popular music scene is now extremely diverse and volatile, and the attempts of the music industry to impose some kind of stability on this, and thereby to secure its profits, are proving increasingly difficult. Of course, this is still about 'consumption': it is about buying records and paying money to dance to records. Yet although 'youth culture' is an inherently commercial phenomenon, the notion of young people as dupes of capitalism, as simply exploited and manipulated, is now very difficult to sustain. As a market for cultural commodities, young people are increasingly unpredictable, constantly shifting, and very hard to reach.[16] There are even those on the political Left who argue that capitalism, the market, actually allows for greater creative opportunities, for more creative participation in culture by the majority of the population, than the official institutions of literature and the other traditional arts.[17] Be that as it may, it is clear that 'youth' can no longer be seen (if indeed it ever could) as a unitary category. On the contrary, it is now highly fragmented—and here the contrast with earlier eras, for example if we look back to the invention or discovery of the teenager as a consumer in the 1950s, is quite striking.

The material I have been referring to here is perhaps a little specialised—although, again, that is partly the point of it. Nevertheless, much of the argument applies equally to the work of performers who are much more popular with younger audiences—obviously to Madonna, but to some extent also to Michael Jackson. In these cases, ambiguity, quotation, if not outright irony, *seem* to be of the essence. The work of these performers should not be seen as self-contained texts, but as commodities which cross the boundaries both between texts and between media.

Nevertheless, there is an obvious risk of determinism here. Focusing on texts alone can easily lead to the assumption either that they contain meanings which are simply imposed on audiences, or alternatively that the characteristics of texts simply reflect the characteristics of audiences. For example, much of the debate about music television—MTV and pop videos—seems to have become stuck at this point.[18] Either there is a form of ideological analysis, which seems to imply that the meanings the critic discovers through close textual analysis are simply swallowed whole by audiences—which clearly makes all sorts of assumptions about how this material is used and read. Or alternatively, there is a kind of postmodern analysis which suggests that the apparently chaotic, allusive style of MTV, its reliance on pastiche and its plundering of cultural resources, somehow reflects the meaningless (or at least rootless) lives of what has come to be termed 'the audiovisual generation'.

The question of how to talk about this kind of material also raises much bigger questions about the role of academic cultural critics, and whom they think they are speaking for. There is a growing tendency for cultural critics to work themselves into paroxysms over the knowingness and complexity of popular culture, while simultaneously believing that their own readings are synonymous with those of audiences in general. The real absence here is of any sustained investigation of what young people themselves actually make of this material, and of the contexts in which it is used and circulated and talked about.

Audiences

So what are the implications of these developments for audiences? Certainly in the case of broadcasting, the institutional and technological changes I have outlined are undoubtedly leading to a fragmentation of the audience. Indeed, we can really no longer talk about a single audience—let alone a mass audience. Video, and increasingly cable and satellite, have meant smaller, more specialised and differentiated audiences. Ultimately, it may not only be the notion of public service that is becoming untenable, but also the notion that the media provide a form of common culture.

The implication here is that we need to look much more concretely and specifically at the diversity of *real* audiences, at subcultures of media users, at the domestic uses of media technology, and the interaction between media use and other social practices and relationships. Indeed, research on media audiences has increasingly moved away from global theories of the mass audience, and from statistical aggregation, towards detailed ethnographic studies—from the mass audience to the socially situated audience.

What emerges very clearly from the research I have been involved in, and the work of some others in the field,[19] is that the singular notion of the audience—and the passivity that term implies—is simply inadequate as a way of explaining young people's use of the media. How children use television, for example, and how they talk about what they watch, need to be considered as social acts with social functions and purposes. The narrow focus on the isolated encounter between the individual child and the all-powerful screen that characterises a great deal of academic research does not begin to do justice to the complexity of this process.

In contrast to the notions of Michael Fallon and others with which I began, this more recent research would suggest that children are far from being simply witless dupes of the media. They do not, for example, mistake the world of the soap operas for reality: on the contrary, even very young children are making complex, differentiated judgments about what is real and what is not, what is realistic or plausible or authentic. Neither, to choose another example, do they accept the messages of TV advertisements in the wholly uncritical way that advertisers might wish: in fact, they are extremely sceptical, indeed often cynical, not merely about the claims that advertisements make about products, but also about the claims they make about the social world. And if you consider the complexity of many of the texts children enjoy, not least the advertisements themselves, there is ample evidence that producers have had to take this on board—although the lesson that you cannot talk down to children is one which has not always been easy to learn.

In the light of popular beliefs about children and television, it remains necessary to argue that children are in fact highly competent, sophisticated viewers—indeed, highly literate viewers. Children are not 'TV zombies', narcotised into mental inertia by television, nor are they ideological victims, simply conditioned into sexism and consumerism and ideology. On the contrary, they actively make their own meanings and use television for their own purposes—and while those purposes are inevitably produced and defined by the culture than surrounds them, they are far from being helpless or passive consumers.

Of course, this does not mean that there are not gaps in children's knowledge, and that there is not room for them to make that knowledge more systematic, and to move beyond it—which is obviously where media education comes in. Nor is it to imply that children are wholly autonomous makers of meaning, able to interpret and use media texts in any way they wish. Clearly, media texts attempt to invite certain kinds of meanings and pleasures, and to discourage others. In effect, they aim to teach the competencies that are required to make sense of them, and they do so in partial and limited ways. These are processes that young people should learn to reflect upon and to analyse. Yet, on the other hand, it is also a problem if this argument appears to sanction rationalistic notions of 'critical reading'—notions which seek to suppress or deny the significant emotional and aesthetic pleasures young people derive from the media, or the considerable cultural investments which may be at stake.

This more situated study of the audience, this emphasis on diversity, on young people's active *use* of the media, coincides with broader social and cultural developments. The notion of the 'postmodern' offers one account of this, or perhaps several. Certainly, what the best accounts of postmodern culture[20] seem to offer is not an abandonment of explanation, or a dissolution of everything into infinite difference and meaninglessness. On the contrary, they provide a detailed account of the economic changes in patterns of work and leisure, in the organisation of production, distribution and exchange, and the cultural implications of those changes. These accounts point to the increasing mobility of post-industrial society, the blurring and breaking down of traditional boundaries, and the dissolution of familiar identities, both at the level of the community and of the nation. But they also identify continuing inequalities of power, not least in terms of traditional categories such as gender, social class and ethnicity.

There are certainly many people who would argue that this fragmentation of the audience is far from being a progressive development—that it is not merely about recognising social diversity, but also about the reconstruction of the individual citizen as an isolated consumer. What some other versions of postmodernism[21] appear to embody is a kind of distorted return to the notion of 'mass society' developed in the early work of the Frankfurt School. What seems to be being argued here—and it is by no means easy to pin it down—is that the media are contributing to a destruction of meaning, a destabilising of reality, in which the notion of the 'social' has itself ceased to be of any relevance.

Perhaps the major problem with this account—and it is one that has been identified by many critics—is one of sufficiency of evidence. What postmodernism often seems to mean is a retreat to mystical theory which precisely fails to engage with the specific cultural developments it is supposedly analysing. Ultimately, I would argue that theoretical notions of 'the end of the social' are of little value in attempting to explain the complex role of popular culture in such developments. By contrast, what emerges from ethnographic studies of media audiences is the idea that popular culture can provide alternative social identities, a sense of place and belonging, particularly for young people, and more particularly for the inner city youth who have been among the most significant victims of right-wing policies. Popular culture, it is argued, offers an 'imagined community', but also a *real* community, albeit one which is not so simply based on locality or on pre-determined social groupings—and this may come to replace the communities which have been ravaged and destroyed. What has emerged in Britain's multi-racial inner cities is what Paul Gilroy[22] has termed a 'syncretic culture', which bridges different ethnic traditions and identifications, yet which takes extremely diverse and specific forms—and to which, one might add, notions of national identity are supremely irrelevant.

In recent years, the debate about audiences in Media Studies seems to have brought to the surface many of the tensions I have been discussing. On the one hand, there has been an increasingly wild and helpless populism, in which all popular culture (particularly the game shows and the wrestling) is seen to be about 'resistance' to 'dominant ideologies', about 'empowerment' of 'the people' and a number of other ill-defined rhetorical terms. On the other hand, there is now a growing reaction against this, and a tendency to lapse into terminal cultural pessimism. Yet although a great deal of intense theoretical heat has been generated here, the empirical basis for the arguments is often extremely limited. Indeed, Media Studies seems to be lapsing into a form of academic theoreticism, in which 'cultural theory' takes precedence over the detailed analysis of empirical data, and is increasingly divorced from cultural and educational practice.

Implications for education

As I have indicated, young people's informal cultural competencies and experiences are at least as complex as ours—even though they may take radically different forms. This is the case in the games they play, in what they read for leisure, in the music they listen to, and in the films and TV programmes they watch. There are certainly continuities with our experiences, even if those continuities may be more apparent to us than they are to them; but there are also considerable qualitative differences, and for the reasons I have outlined these are only likely to increase.

These differences are partly a result of technological developments—in particular, the growth of 'interactive' media—and of some profound institutional changes in terms of how media texts are produced and circulated. This seems to be leading, albeit in a limited way, to a blurring of distinctions between production and consumption, and a sense in which traditional top-down models of *mass* communication—of one sender and many receivers—seem no longer to apply. It also seems to be having an impact on the kinds of material children are exposed to and appear to enjoy—and again we can detect here a shifting or blurring of boundaries, between texts, between genres and between media. These developments in turn reflect much more fundamental social and cultural changes—which might broadly be defined as a matter of changing relationships between the centre and the periphery, in which notions such as public service or common culture seem to be much harder to sustain. At the same time, these developments would also seem to make possible new cultural and communicative competencies—new forms of literacy. And to ignore them is to ignore something that is not only self-evidently important, but that may well prove to be of great educational value.

This has important implications for the English curriculum. It involves abandoning the notion that English is primarily about defending 'high culture', and inoculating children against the influence of 'popular culture'. We need to begin by recognising that for the vast majority of people, traditional elite high culture is simply an irrelevance: it is not part of their experience and is unlikely to become part of it, however many anthologies and compulsory Shakespeare plays we may attempt to force them to read. We need to begin by looking at where young people do find meaning and identity, at their existing cultural activities, rather than seeking to replace these with something we regard as better for them, or that we arrogantly assume makes them more 'human'. This is not to suggest that we simply replace 'literature' with 'popular culture', but that we need to develop a more rigorous, and less defensive, approach to teaching about the whole range of cultural products and experiences. In the process, the ways in which cultural products are categorised, and the social functions that judgements of cultural value are seen to perform, will inevitably have to be open to questioning and analysis.

The version of English contained in the existing National Curriculum documents does not consistently adopt this defensive approach, although it is certainly marked by a considerable degree of confusion, not least in its definition of 'literature' itself. Nevertheless, the Cox Report and the existing

National Curriculum go a long way to acknowledging the importance of media education—and to that extent, they reflect something that has been part of most English teachers' practice for many decades. Yet even here, the broader potential of media education has largely been neglected. While it seems to be acceptable to ask the kinds of questions I have raised in this paper in relation to media texts—for example, about institutions, about representation and about audiences—there is very little sense of their being extended to the study of 'literature'. Furthermore, in placing a central emphasis on *factual* media, the National Curriculum continues to neglect the fictional media that are so central to young people's lives.

In my view, this reflects a continuing anxiety about popular culture which is apparent even in many 'progressive' versions of English teaching. In emphasising the relevance and validity of each child's culture, language and self-expression, progressive English has nevertheless often tended to adopt a sentimental approach to working class and 'ethnic' cultures. In searching for an 'authentic' culture that offers continuity and values, it has tried to recast those cultures in the image of the dominant culture. At the same time, the 'mass-produced' cultures of the media have been condemned as merely 'inauthentic', along with the complex and diverse ways in which audiences use and appropriate them. Of course, the major problem here has always been: how do we define 'authenticity', and how do we recognise it when we see it? Cultural Studies has increasingly questioned the distinctions between 'folk culture' and 'mass culture' on which such arguments are often based; and for many observers of 'postmodern culture', the current context is one in which the notion of authenticity itself has become increasingly irrelevant.[23]

As I have argued, media education offers a more rigorous theoretical basis for enabling young people to understand and to participate in the most important means of communication in modern societies. It explicitly addresses the kinds of questions I have raised here, about cultural production and social power, and about the relations between technologies, institutions, texts and audiences. It does not seek merely to validate or celebrate students' cultural experiences—even assuming that they need us to validate them in the first place. While media education begins with what young people already know, it also seeks to enable them to reflect upon that knowledge, to make it systematic, and to move beyond it.

David Buckingham

In recent years, media education has had to come to terms with its own historical legacy, and to address some complex questions about students' learning. It has begun to abandon a merely defensive position, in which young people are seen as 'dupes' of media ideologies, and teachers as the agents of 'demystification'. The notion of media education as an evangelical crusade—a means of saving children from the media—has given way to a more effective approach, which builds upon the pedagogic strengths of progressive English teaching, while emphasising the central importance of analysis and reflection. In this more recent version of media education, practical media production and critical analysis are of equal importance: understanding is seen to arise, not merely from the 'transmission' of academic knowledge, but from the reflexive and dialectical relationship between 'theory' and 'practice'.[24]

The developments I have described in this paper will certainly lead to further changes in media education. Both in production *and* analytical work, they would seem to offer exciting new possibilities. The increasing accessibility of the new media production technologies—and in the near future, of multi-media—means that practical work is both cheaper and easier to 'manage' in the classroom. But the interactive capacities of these technologies also offer much greater possibilities for analytical work— enabling students to manipulate images and texts and to see the consequences of what they have done. This may offer an approach to analysis which is much less cut-and-dried, much more genuinely exploratory, than media education often is.

More broadly, media education will need to move beyond its traditional focus on analysis or deconstruction of the text. As I have argued, the boundaries between texts and between media have become increasingly blurred. The case for an approach to teaching and to research that begins with the audience, and with questions of social circulation and use, rather than with the text, is an increasingly powerful one.

Ultimately, we may be moving towards a situation in which the media classroom can genuinely become a site of cultural production, in which the aim is to enable students to build upon their existing informal cultural competencies, rather than seeking to replace them with something which we as teachers define as more ideologically correct. This is not in any sense to argue that we simply leave students where they are—or even that we engage in some kind of celebration of 'their' culture. It is simply to suggest that if we want to encourage students to understand and to participate in the culture that surrounds them, we need to begin by taking that culture seriously and seeking to understand it ourselves.

Conclusion

In this paper, I have argued for a broader notion of literacy—a notion which is concerned with cultural and communicative competencies, irrespective of the medium in which they are exercised, and which therefore necessarily includes the competencies which are developed in relationship to the so-called 'new' media. I have also argued for a view of literacy which sees it in social, cultural and political terms, and not simply as a set of technical or intellectual skills. And I have argued for a form of education— within the school subjects of English and of media education—that values and builds upon those cultural competencies, rather than seeking to invalidate them in favour of some narrow and divisive notion of cultural value, or indeed of ideological value. It is a form of education which is both rigorous and challenging, and which seeks to equip students for the social and technological changes that lie ahead.

Current moves to revise the English curriculum would seem to be moving steadfastly in the opposite direction. Increasingly, policy makers appear to have abandoned the consensual middle ground, in favour of an approach that seems determined to turn the clock back to a mythical pre-modern era. The notion that the curriculum might equip students for the challenges of an increasingly technological, media-oriented society—not merely in the field of leisure, but also in the 'world of work'—seems to have been all but abandoned. With their insistence on an atrophied literary canon, and their neglect of the cultural experiences and competencies of the vast majority of young people, these developments will merely result in irrelevance and incoherence. The social, cultural and technological changes that await us in the next decade will *inevitably* require a much more profound rethinking of our conception of literacy, and of education itself.

David Buckingham

Notes and References

An earlier version of this paper was presented at the *'Domains of Literacy'* Conference held at the Institute of Education in September 1992. The author would like to thank Celia Greenwood and Julian Sefton-Green for their comments.

1. *The Sun*, 14 May 1991.
2. *'The Cultural Dimension in Education'*, speech delivered to the National Foundation of Arts Education, London, 20 November 1992.
3. Willis, P. (1990) *Common Culture: Symbolic Work at Play in the Everyday Cultures of the Young*, Milton Keynes, Open University Press. The figures that follow are taken from Willis, and from the journal *Cultural Trends*.
4. For recent work in this field, see Cary Bazalgette, (1991) *Media Education*, London, Hodder and Stoughton; Manuel Alvarado and Oliver Boyd-Barrett (1992) (eds.), *Media Education: An Introduction*, London, British Film Institute; David Buckingham (1990) (ed.), *Watching Media Learning: Making Sense of Media Education*, London, Falmer Press.
5. For a detailed discussion of this issue, see David Buckingham, (1989) 'Television Literacy: A Critique', *Radical Philosophy* 51.
6. Williams, R. (1974) *Television: Technology and Cultural Form*, Glasgow, Fontana.
7. Williams, *Television*, op. cit.
8. The first of these tendencies is represented in the work of Adorno: e.g. Theodor Adorno and Max Horkheimer, (1991) *The Dialectics of Enlightenment*, London, Routledge. For examples of the second, see Walter Benjamin, (1976) 'The work of art in the age of mechanical reproduction', in *Illuminations*, London, Cape; and Hans Magnus Enzensberger, 'Constituents of a theory of the media', in Denis McQuail (1972) (ed.), *Sociology of Mass Communications*, Harmondsworth, Penguin.
9. This notion of the public sphere derives from the work of Jurgen Habermas, e.g. *The Structural Transformation of the Public Sphere*, Cambridge, Polity, (1989); see also the discussion in John B. Thompson, (1990) *Ideology and Modern Culture*, Cambridge, Polity. Examples of this critique in relation to television may be found in Nicholas Garnham, (1991) *Capitalism and Communication*, London, Sage, and Marjorie Ferguson (1990) (ed.), *Public Communications: The New Imperatives*, London, Sage.
10. See Willis, op. cit.; David Buckingham, 'Media education and the media industries: bridging the gaps?', *British Journal of Education and Work*, forthcoming 1993.

11 See Lisa Lewis (1992) (ed.), *The Adoring Audience*, London, Routledge; and Henry Jenkins, (1992) *Textual Poachers: Television Fans and Participatory Culture*, London, Routledge.
12 See Dick Hebdige, 'Towards a cartography of taste 1935-1962', in B. Waites, T. Bennett and G. Martin (1982) (eds.), *Popular Culture Past and Present*, London, Croom Helm/Open University Press.
13 For a useful discussion of this issue, see Charlotte Brunsdon, (1990) 'Problems with quality', *Screen* 31(1), pp. 67-90.
14 For a thought-provoking account of this area, see Marsha Kinder, (1991) *Playing with Power in Movies, Television and Video Games*, Berkeley, University of California.
15 See the contributions by Martin Barker and Julian Sefton-Green to David Buckingham (1993) (ed.), *Reading Audiences: Young People and the Media*, Manchester, Manchester University Press.
16 See Mica Nava, (1992) *Changing Cultures: Youth, Culture and Consumerism*, London, Sage.
17 For example, Paul Willis, op. cit.
18 For example, E. Ann Kaplan, (1987) *Rocking Around the Clock*, London, Methuen; and Andrew Goodwin, (1987) 'Music video in the (post) modern world', *Screen* 28 (3).
19 David Buckingham, (1993) *Children Talking Television: The Making of Television Literacy*, London, Falmer, and *Reading Audiences*, op. cit.; also Bob Hodge and David Tripp, (1986) *Children and Television: A Semiotic Approach*, Cambridge, Polity.
20 For example, the work of David Harvey, (1989) *The Condition of Postmodernity*, Oxford, Blackwell.
21 See, for example, Jean Baudrillard, (1988) *Selected Writings*, Cambridge, Polity; and, among many critiques, Christopher Norris, (1990) 'Lost in the funhouse: Baudrillard and the politics of postmodernism', in Roy Boyne and Ali Rattansi (eds.), *Postmodernism and Society*, London, Macmillan.
22 Gilroy, (1987) *There Ain't No Black in the Union Jack*, London, Hutchinson. See also Simon Jones, (1988) *Black Culture, White Youth*, London, Macmillan.
23 This issue has been explored in some detail in studies of popular music: see, for example, Richard Middleton, (1990) *Studying Popular Music*, Milton Keynes, Open University Press; and Steve Redhead, (1990) *The End-of-the-Century Party: Youth and Pop Towards 2000*, Manchester, Manchester University Press.
24 See David Buckingham, *Watching Media Learning*, op. cit.; and David Buckingham and Julian Sefton-Green, *Cultural Studies Goes to School: Reading and Teaching Popular Culture*, London, Falmer, forthcoming.

Partnership in teacher training: Talk and chalk
Clare Hake

Learning on the job will not produce teachers who can reflect on, compare, and thereby improve their practice. Clare Hake applauds the recent shift in emphasis towards more school-based teacher training, but argues that university departments of education can and must make a continuing contribution to training. In the space created by a partnership between school and college, students can conduct 'an active and rational exploration of the task of teaching'. Using her own experience first as a mentor for trainee teachers in school, and later as a university curriculum tutor, Clare Hake describes and illustrates the advantages of the partnership between school and college exemplified by the Oxford University teacher training scheme. School experience may be paramount but impoverished without the opportunity for reflection provided by such a partnership.

ISBN 1 872767 46 X   36 pp   paperback   £3.95

A market-led alternative for the curriculum: Breaking the code
James Tooley

The National Curriculum is a national disaster. But there appears to be a consensus that a national curriculum of some kind is desirable. James Tooley challenges this consensus, and argues radically that curricula should be entrusted to the market. Reviewing the arguments for a national curriculum, he concludes that a cumbersome, costly, unreliable and ultimately unnecessary, national system should be abandoned and market forces should be allowed to operate. He argues that a market-led curriculum would be liberating, empowering and facilitate egalitarian ideas far better than any bureaucratised, centralised curriculum.

ISBN 1 872767 51 6   42 pp   paperback   £3.95

Education and the crisis in values: should we be philosophical about it?
Graham Haydon

'Education should seek to impart moral values'—what does this mean? *Does* society face a moral crisis? Does the increasingly public expression of a plurality of moral values signal a decline or an advance? Can education help us with the plurality of values with which we have to live? Graham Haydon addresses these complex issues, arguing that philosophy *can* both help us to understand the current crisis in values and to deal with it. While philosophy may not provide teachers with a lifeline for survival in the classroom, philosophers just might prove to be swimming instructors. Philosophy need not be remote from popular understanding, and should be brought more fully into the training of teachers and into the curriculum of our children to provide this necessary support

ISBN 1 872767 56 7   25 pp   paperback   £3.95

The aims of school history: The National Curriculum and beyond
Peter Lee, John Slater, Paddy Walsh and John White with a preface by Denis Shemilt

Why is it important to include history in the school curriculum? Is it because the subject (and its methodology) is so profoundly educative that it can be engaged in for its own sake? Or should the study of the past be harnessed to purposes such as preparation for democratic citizenship? These and other questions highlighted by the introduction of the National Curriculum are discussed here by historians and philosophers. The result is a lively and stimulating debate that has important implications for the future of school history.
ISBN 1 872767 26 5   55 pp   paperback   £4.50

Time to change the 1981 Education Act
Brahm Norwich

Brahm Norwich reviews the workings of the 1981 Education Act and how far the special education provision it was intended to enhance has been affected by the 1988 Education Act and subsequent developments. He argues for a reassessment of the definition of special educational need and for tightening the link between assessment of need and provision. Concern for the protection of provision on changing circumstances also prompts him to recommend that duties placed on local education authorities by the 1981 Act should be now extended to school governing bodies, and that parents should have the choice of a quicker form of decision making.
ISBN 1 872767 36 2   36 pp   paperback   £3.95

The promise and perils of educational comparison
Martin McLean

Can Britain's relatively poor economic performance be blamed on its inferior schools and teaching? Politicians in recent years have increasingly supported their proposals for educational reform with examples of practice in other countries. Against this background Martin McLean examines the uses and possible abuses of the discipline of comparative education. He illustrates his argument with many possible examples, concluding that the challenge to those who turn to other systems of education to find support for their arguments is whether they can let their thinking 'take in deeper and wider perspectives and whether they can accept the conclusions that emerge'.
ISBN 1 872767 31 1   40 pp   paperback   £3.95

National Curriculum science: So near and yet so far
Arthur Jennings

When the first proposals for the National Curriculum science were published in 1988 the goal of giving all pupils a broad and exciting experience of science seemed to be within reach. Arthur Jennings traces here the history of implementation and asks whether, under pressure of accommodating a workable system of assessment, that original goal has not been lost. Teachers will need to be vigilant, he urges, and carry parents and school governors with them, if they are to go beyond teaching 'to the tests' and achieve a real experience of science for all.
ISBN 1 872767 41 9   41 pp   paperback   £3.95

The arts 5-16: Changing the agenda
John White

John White critically examines the central issues that underlie the National Curriculum Council's document *The Arts 5-16: A curriculum framework*. Education in the arts has lacked a coherent sense of purpose and whilst the NCC has tried to provide an integrated policy it has paid insufficient attention to the underlying aims of education in the arts. In addressing this problem John White presents a searching discussion of the purposes and underlying assumptions of education in the arts and their practical realisation. His concern is to ensure that the foundations for work in school in the arts are secure and defensible and above all will generate a love of art.
ISBN 1 872767 06 0   38 pp   paperback   £3.95

More has meant women: the feminisation of schooling
Jane Miller

'To an extent that is quite inadequately recognised, state education is provided by women; as is virtually all schooling, whether public or private, for young children.' Jane Miller argues that criticism of current educational practice often has gender as its hidden target. She draws on historical evidence and on her own teaching experience to develop a complex and provocative discussion.
ISBN 1 872767 21 4   31 pp   paperback   £3.95

Music education and the National Curriculum
Keith Swanwick

Keith Swanwick discusses the evolution of music education in schools and critically examines the implications of the attainment targets in the National Curriculum. On the central question of music as knowledge he considers that the National Curriculum Working Group put a misplaced emphasis on factual information and quantity. Knowing about and understanding music is much more than processing factual information and any form of assessment must recognise *qualitative* awareness rather than acquisition of *quantitative* facts. Swanwick's improved criteria for assessment have in part been accepted by the Secretary of State for Education. In this strongly argued work Swanwick seeks to identify a way forward for music in the classroom that would secure the confidence of musicians and music educators.
ISBN 1 872767 11 7   33 pp   paperback   £3.95

the Tufnell Press
47 Dalmeny Road,
London, N7 0DY

ORDER FORM

Please send me the following:

	Price	Quantity	Total

Total amount enclosed _____

Please make cheques payable to the Tufnell Press

NAME _____

ADDRESS _____

_____

_____

INS12/1993